Birds

Poems by
JUDITH WRIGHT

Introduced by Meredith McKinney

National Library of Australia

Published by the National Library of Australia
Canberra ACT 2600 Australia

Poems © Meredith McKinney 2000
Introduction © Meredith McKinney 2003
This compilation © National Library of Australia 2003
Reprinted 2004, 2010

National Library of Australia Cataloguing-in-Publication entry

Wright, Judith, 1915–2000.
Birds : poems.

New ed.
ISBN 0 642 10774 2.

I. McKinney, Meredith, 1950–. II. National Library of Australia.
 Pictures Collection. III. Title.

A821.3

Edited by Paul Cliff
Cover design by Noel Wendtman
Internal design by Kathy Jakupec

Printed in China through The Australian Book Connection

Front cover and title page images: see pages 11 and 48

For Meredith

Editorial Note

For this new edition of *Birds*—the fourth to appear since 1962, and commemorating 25 years since the volume's most recent appearance in 1978—the publishers, in consultation with Meredith McKinney, have chosen to incorporate six additional poems.

These supplementary poems are: 'Birds' (p. 1), an early piece from *The Gateway* (1953); 'Camping at Split Rock' (p. 70), from *The Other Half* (1966); 'Oriole, Oriole', 'Lament for Passenger Pigeons' and 'Reminiscence' (pp. 73, 74 and 76), from *Alive* (1973); and 'Seasonal Flocking' (p. 78), from the poet's final collection, *Phantom Dwelling* (1985).

Acknowledgments

Birds was originally published by Angus & Robertson Australia, in 1962. Second edition 1967. Third edition 1978.

Permission to reproduce the poems here is kindly granted by Meredith McKinney; HarperCollins Australia (*Collected Poems 1942–1985*, 1994); and Tom Thompson of ETT Imprint (*A Human Pattern: Selected Poems*, 1996).

Illustrations: The National Library thanks Stephen Iredale (for estate of Lilian Medland), Margaret McCredie (for estate of Hardy Wilson), William T. Cooper, Viola Temple Watts and Jacqueline Mitelman for use of images in this book. (For information on illustrators, see 'Notes on the Artists', p. 80.)

Jacqueline Mitelman
Portrait of Judith Wright 1988
nla.pic–an13145657

Contents

E.E. (Ebenezer Edward) Gostelow (1867–1944)
The Little Lorikeet and Purple-Crowned Lorikeet (Glossopsitta pusilla and G. porphyrocephala) 1928
nla.pic-an3922589

Birds

Whatever the bird is, is perfect in the bird.
Weapon kestrel hard as a blade's curve,
thrush round as a mother or a full drop of water,
fruit-green parrot wise in his shrieking swerve—
all are what bird is and do not reach beyond bird.

Whatever the bird does is right for the bird to do—
cruel kestrel dividing in his hunger the sky,
thrush in the trembling dew beginning to sing,
parrot clinging and quarrelling and veiling his queer eye—
all these are as birds are and good for birds to do.

But I am torn and beleaguered by my own people.
The blood that feeds my heart is the blood they gave me,
and my heart is the house where they gather and fight for dominion—
all different, all with a wish and a will to save me,
to turn me into the ways of other people.

If I could leave their battleground for the forest of a bird
I could melt the past, the present and the future in one
and find the words that lie behind all these languages.
Then I could fuse my passions into one clear stone
and be simple to myself as the bird is to the bird.

— From *The Gateway*, 1953

1

Introduction

'Whatever the bird is, is perfect in the bird', says Judith Wright (1915 – 2000) in her poem 'Birds'. The poems of this present volume not only offer intimate portraits of many of the birds that were dear to her, but each poem in its varied way reaches to touch each varied bird's 'perfection'. They are the poet's way of becoming one with the creatures she loved.

The poems that form the core of this book, first collected into the volume *Birds* (Angus & Robertson, 1962), were written when I was a child. Many of them were read to me when my mother first wrote them, often while we sat at the sunny breakfast table with the birds flashing brilliantly down to the windowsill beside us for bread, or quarrelling in the loquat tree beyond, as she read. Others were written for maturer ears than mine, and emerged from more private and imaginatively intense encounters with birds. Reading this volume, we experience a kind of wing flicker—from light and delighting, to darker tones, and back to light again —as each bird and each poem settles for a moment in the mind.

The poems originally collected in *Birds* were written during the 1950s, the first decade of Judith's time of living and writing surrounded by the lush rainforest world of Tamborine Mountain in south-east Queensland, and most come directly out of that world and time. This was the happiest decade of her life, when she at last felt she had truly come into her own as poet, lover and mother, and the abundance of Tamborine's natural world and its birds spoke back to her of her own sense of abundance and delight. This place and its happiness felt the more intense for her in its contrast with much of her earlier life.

Judith's early experience both of life and of the natural world had been rather different. She was born, and grew up, in a colder and more difficult world, the 'clean, lean, hungry' landscape of the

New England tableland, over the border to Brisbane's south. Her childhood was spent learning to love and find herself through this place of 'bony trees wincing under the winter', where 'wind and frost in the black sallies / roughen the sleek-haired slopes'. New England, in her memory, was the harsh clarity and hard edges of a winter landscape, the difficulties of early years overshadowed by the long illness and death of her mother, and herself an intense, sometimes unhappy, occasionally ecstatic young girl who poured herself into her poetry. Childhood memories and the New England landscape are drawn on for some of these bird poems, such as 'Eggs and Nestlings' (p. 12), 'Black Cockatoos' (p. 46), and 'Rainbow-bird' (p. 49).

Judith was in her early 30s when she moved to Tamborine. She had met my father, the philosopher and playwright Jack McKinney, when she came to Brisbane several years earlier. There seems never to have been any question in their minds that they belonged together. The situation, however, was full of difficulty—although Jack and his wife had parted ways, divorce remained beyond his grasp owing to the nature of the law at that time, when mutual consent was still a prerequisite. (Judith and Jack were finally able to marry two years before his death, in 1964, when the law changed.) Brisbane was not a place where one could openly flaunt an extra-marital relationship. The constant need for secrecy, and the impasse that dogged the relationship, sometimes drove them both close to despair. Finally, they managed to buy a tiny, rather primitive two-room cottage in what was in those days the relatively hidden little world of Tamborine. Jack moved there alone, to live and write, while Judith kept her job in the city and visited secretly at weekends. But eventually her longing for Jack, and for a child, drove her to throw caution to the wind.

By the late 1940s, Judith was beginning to be widely known as a poet. It was time to turn her back on compromise, and to devote herself to what she loved—to Jack and to poetry. In 1948 she gave up her city job, and under the guise of 'Mrs McKinney' moved in to live with him and to write, and Tamborine became her home. Two years later, she bore a child (myself).

The ensuing decade when these poems were written was thus for Judith a precious and dearly-won time of warmth and bounty to counterbalance at last what felt in contrast like the chilly dearth and difficulty of her earlier years. And the subtropical bounty of Tamborine's lush natural world embodied her experience, as many poems of this period attest. She wrote poems of the rainforest, of its plants and flowers—and of its birds.

Many of these poems have a newly relaxed, almost conversational tone and rhythm, an often humorous ease and an intimacy of voice that surely reflects the new intimacies and joys of her life. Many are simple and straightforward poems, and I remember delighting in them as a child when she read them to me. ('The Swamp Pheasant', p. 18, which featured our battered old tomcat Violet, was my favourite.) Yet for all their lightness of touch, each poem seeks to somehow convey the essence of the bird's character. These poems are not just about the birds: they seek, in their varying voices and rhythms as well as in their images, to somehow be that bird, to embody it. The magpies who saunter down the road 'with hands in pockets, left and right', or the very different black cockatoos 'tossed on the crest / of their high trees, crying the world's unrest', are each instantly and deeply recognisable. I think it is that recognition which delighted me as a child, and which I still find delightful.

Within this volume, poems such as 'The Swamp Pheasant' (p. 18), 'Parrots' (p. 32), 'Lyrebirds' (p. 54), 'Satin Bower-birds' (p. 56), and 'Brush Turkey' (p. 58), speak directly from my mother's personal experience of watching the birds around our house, or walking the rainforest paths nearby—places alive with birds both seen and unseen. Others—'Black Swans' (p. 51) and 'Pelicans' (p. 41) in particular—are of birds that we grew to know well in those years from extended stays in our small holiday cottage on the lake at Boreen Point, not far from Noosa. Poems such as 'Egrets' (p. 24), 'Apostle-birds' (p. 31) and 'Camping at Split Rock' (p. 70) come from the weeks-long camping holidays that we regularly took in our little Austin panel van, slowly wandering back roads and camping wherever we fancied along the way.

My mother's love of birds led her to many encounters with them, some of which are commemorated in these poems. She was always rescuing wounded birds, and we would commonly have at least one of them recuperating about the house. The poem 'Currawong' (p. 16), with its fond description of a bird which so many dislike, was originally addressed to a particularly tenacious young currawong (named simply 'Bird') that she reared from infancy, and which refused to leave her even after it had learned to fly. It would sit on her shoulder wherever she went, and defend her against all who approached—including on occasion my father and myself. 'Wounded Night-bird' (p. 37) is also a poem that has its origin in a moment I remember well, when a wounded night-jar that Judith had rescued by our front gate bit her to the bone in its terror.

'Wounded Night-bird' well illustrates the fact that many of these poems deal also in very serious matters. It is not simply a poem about a painful encounter with a frightened bird—it is a poem in which the poet finds herself confronting and battling far deeper primal terrors, through the blazing circuit of fear that suddenly joins her to the bird's terror as she holds it. As this poem reveals, for all her delight in birds Judith's vision of their world, and of her own, was shaped by a darker knowledge.

The experiences of cruelty, pain and death are as inseparable from the lives of birds as they are from those of humans, and poems such as 'Winter Kestrel' (p. 15), 'Black-shouldered Kite' (p. 23), 'Migrant Swift' (p. 28), and 'Rainbow-bird' (p. 49) look steadily at this darker side. Ultimately, as the poet says in "Dove—Love" (p. 26), to look deeply at birds is to enter a world that 'also rhymes with us'. 'Extinct Birds' (p. 66) brings this theme full circle, to end the *Birds* volume with a sorrowing and clear-sighted gaze turned on the terrible damage we have done, and continue to do, to our world even as we love it.

This is a theme that carried through directly from these earlier decades until Judith's death in Canberra in 2000, at the age of 85, and it finds its full poetic statement in the later 'Lament for Passenger Pigeons' included here (p. 74). In the decade after these poems were written, Judith came to focus her energies increasingly on the crucial, and in those days still largely unrecognised, need for environmental awareness. With a few friends, she helped found one of the earliest nature conservation movements, and she remained an active and dedicated environmentalist for the rest of her life—indeed her name today is associated as much with the environment movement and the Aboriginal rights movement as it is with poetry. In the poems of *Birds*, we can trace the deep responsiveness and love of the natural world that were the seeds from which this later shift in Judith's life emerged.

At the end of her life, as in her early years, my mother continued to live surrounded by birds. Her last few decades were spent in a colder and sparer natural world than that of Tamborine Mountain—the southern tablelands country near the town of Braidwood in New South Wales, which she said reminded her of her New England childhood. Here, on the 100 acres (40 ha) of snowgum country that was her home, the birdbath by her door was still thronged with many of the same birds that inhabit these earlier poems—blue wrens, black cockatoos, parrots and thornbills among many others.

As she slowed into old age, her delight in birds—and in life generally—grew, if anything, keener. 'Fallen leaves on the current scarcely move', she wrote in a late poem ('Dust', *Phantom Dwelling*), that contemplates both the river below her house and her own ageing self—'but the azure kingfisher flashes upriver still'.

MEREDITH MCKINNEY
Braidwood, New South Wales, 2003

The Peacock

Shame on the aldermen who locked
the Peacock in a dirty cage!
His blue and copper sheens are mocked
by habit, hopelessness and age.

The weary Sunday families
along their gravelled paths repeat
the pattern of monotonies
that he treads out with restless feet.

And yet the Peacock shines alone;
and if one metal feather fall
another grows where that was grown.
Love clothes him still, in spite of all.

How pure the hidden spring must rise
that time and custom cannot stain!
It speaks its joy again—again.
Perhaps the aldermen are wise.

Lionel Lindsay (1874–1961)
The White Peacock c.1925
nla.pic-an10933943

The Blue Wrens and the Butcher-bird

Sweet and small the blue wren
whistles to his gentle hen,
"The creek is full, the day is gold,
the tale of love is never told.
Fear not, my love, nor fly away,
for safe, safe in the blackthorn-tree
we shall build our nest today.
Trust to me, oh trust to me."

Cobwebs they gather and dry grass,
greeting each other as they pass
up to the nest and down again,
the blue wren and the brown wren.
They seek and carry far and near,
down the bank and up the hill,
until that crystal note they hear
that strikes them dumb and holds them still.

Great glorious passion of a voice—
sure all that hear it must rejoice.
But in the thorn-bush silent hide
the nest-builders side by side.
"The blue-wren's nestlings and his wife,
and he himself, that sprig of blue,
I shall kill, and hang them safe—
the blackthorn spears shall run them through."

Still and still the blue wren
sits beside his cowering hen.
There they wait like stone by stone
until the butcher-bird is gone.
Then soft and sweet the blue wren
twitters to his anxious hen,
"Trust to me, oh trust to me;
I know another blackthorn-tree."

Neville H. Cayley (1853–1903)
Blue Wren 1892
nla.pic-an6928686

Eggs and Nestlings

The moss-rose and the palings made
a solemn and a waiting shade
where eagerly the mother pressed
a sheltering curve into her nest.

Her tranced eye, her softened stare,
warned me when I saw her there,
and perfect as the grey nest's round,
three frail and powdered eggs I found.

My mother called me there one day.
Beneath the nest the eggshells lay,
and in it throbbed the triple greed
of one incessant angry need.

Those yellow gapes, those starveling cries,
how they disquieted my eyes!—
the shapeless furies come to be
from shape's most pure serenity.

Neville H. Cayley (1853–1903)
Magpies Feeding Young 1893
nla.pic-an6942168

Lilian Medland (1880–1955)
Nankeen Kestrel; detail from *Falco longipennis and Other Birds* 1930s
nla.pic-an14238600

Winter Kestrel

Fierce with hunger and cold
all night in the windy tree
the kestrel to the sun cries,
"Oh bird in the egg of the sea,

"break out, and tower, and hang
high, oh most high,
and watch for the running mouse
with your unwearying eye;

"and I shall hover and hunt,
and I shall see him move,
and I like a bolt of power
shall seize him from above.

"Break from your blue shell,
you burning Bird or God,
and light me to my kill—
and you shall share his blood."

Currawong

The currawong has shallow eyes—
bold shallow buttons of yellow glass
that see all round his sleek black skull.
Small birds sit quiet when he flies;
mothers of nestlings cry *Alas!*
He is a gangster, his wife's a moll.

But I remember long ago
(a child beside the seldom sea)
the currawongs as wild as night
quarrelling, talking, crying so,
in the scarlet-tufted coral-tree;
and past them that blue stretch of light,

the ocean with its dangerous song.
Robber then and robber still,
he cries now with the same strange word
(currawong—currawong)
that from those coxcomb trees I heard.
Take my bread and eat your fill,
bold, cruel and melodious bird.

E.E. (Ebenezer Edward) Gostelow (1867–1944)
Black-Winged Currawang (i.e. Currawong) 1937
nla.pic–an3816563

The Swamp Pheasant

The swamp pheasant was wide awake
when the dawn-star came up new.
He scrambled up the garden gate
and made green tracks in the web-white dew.

All round the lawn he ran and peered;
he found a lizard under a stone;
he found a tiny wart-eyed toad—
one scuffle and it was gone.

Then out came our cat Violet,
one eye half-closed from many a fight.
He combed from his whisker a mouse's fur,
and breathed the air with calm delight.

The swamp pheasant looks and sees
a tiger made in pheasant-size—
runs to the fence and scrambles out,
while Violet squints his scornful eyes.

And I lean out and laugh to see
that queer old woman cross the street,
holding her brown skirts high behind
and scuttling on her long black feet.

E.E. (Ebenezer Edward) Gostelow (1867–1944)

Pheasant Coucal or Swamp Pheasant (Centropus phasianinus) 1932

nla.pic-an3813701

Thornbills

Their tiny torrent of flight
sounds in the trees like rain,
flicking the leaves to the light—
a scattered handful of grain,
the thornbills little as bees.

I hear in the blowing trees
the sudden tune of their song.
Pray that the hawk not sees,
who has scanned the wind so long
for his small living food.

Oh let no enemies
drink the quick wine of blood
that leaps in their pulse of praise.
Wherever a trap is set
may they slip through the mesh of the net.
Nothing should do them wrong.

Betty Temple Watts (1901–1992)
Detail from *Thornbills, Warblers and Chats* 1958–1967
nla.pic-an6940276-22

Lilian Medland (1880-1955)
Detail from *Falco longipennis and Other Birds* 1930s
nla.pic-an14238600

Black-shouldered Kite

Carved out of strength, the furious kite
shoulders off the wind's hate.
The black mark that bars his white
is the pride and hunger of Cain.
Perfect, precise, the angry calm
of his closed body, that snow-storm—
of his still eye that threatens harm.
Hunger and force his beauty made
and turned a bird to a knife-blade.

Egrets

Once as I travelled through a quiet evening,
I saw a pool, jet-black and mirror-still.
Beyond, the slender paperbarks stood crowding;
each on its own white image looked its fill,
and nothing moved but thirty egrets wading—
thirty egrets in a quiet evening.

Once in a lifetime, lovely past believing,
your lucky eyes may light on such a pool.
As though for many years I had been waiting,
I watched in silence, till my heart was full
of clear dark water, and white trees unmoving,
and, whiter yet, those thirty egrets wading.

E.E. (Ebenezer Edward) Gostelow (1867–1944)
White Egret (Egretta alba) 1938
nla.pic–an3821510

"Dove—Love"

The dove purrs—over and over the dove
purrs its declaration. The wind's tone
changes from tree to tree, the creek on stone
alters its sob and fall, but still the dove
goes insistently on, telling its love
    "I could eat you."

And in captivity, they say, doves do.
Gentle, methodical, starting with the feet
(the ham-pink succulent toes
on their thin stems of rose),
baring feather by feather the wincing meat:
    "I could eat you."

That neat suburban head, that suit of grey,
watchful conventional eye and manicured claw—
these also rhyme with us. The doves play
on one repetitive note that plucks the raw
helpless nerve, their soft "I do. I do.
    I could eat you."

Betty Temple Watts (1901–1992)

Pigeons and Doves 1958–1967

nla.pic-an6940276-5

Migrant Swift

Beneath him slid the furrows of the sea;
against his sickle-skill the air divided;
he used its thrust and current easily.

He trusted all to air: the flesh that bred him
was worn against it to a blade-thin curving
made all for flight; air's very creatures fed him.

Such pride as this, once fallen, there's no saving.
Whatever struck him snapped his stretch of wing.
He came to earth at last, Icarus diving.

Like a contraption of feathers, bone and string,
his storm-blue wings hung useless. Yet his eyes
lived in his wreckage—head still strove to rise
and turn towards the lost impossible spring.

Betty Temple Watts (1901–1992)

Swifts, Swallows and Martins 1958–1967

nla.pic-an24895910

E.E. (Ebenezer Edward) Gostelow (1867–1944)

Apostle Bird (Struthidea cinerea) 1933

nla.pic-an3779018

Apostle-birds

Strangers are easily put out of countenance,
and we were strangers in that place;
camped among trees we had no names for;
not knowing the local customs.

And those big grey birds, how they talked about us!
They hung head-down from branches and peered.
They spread their tawny wings like fans,
and came so close we could have touched them;
staring with blunt amusement.
It was ridiculous to feel embarrassed.

Of that camp I remember the large wild violets,
the sound of the creek on stones,
the wind-combed grass, the tree-trunks
wrinkled and grey like elephant-legs all round us;
and those apostle-birds, so rude to strangers,
so self-possessed and clannish,
we were glad when they flew away.

Parrots

Loquats are cold as winter suns.
Among rough leaves their clusters glow
like oval beads of cloudy amber,
or small fat flames of birthday candles.

Parrots, when the winter dwindles
their forest fruits and seeds, remember
where the swelling loquats grow,
how chill and sweet their thin juice runs,

and shivering in the morning cold
we draw the curtains back and see
the lovely greed of their descending,
the lilt of flight that blurs their glories,

and warm our eyes upon the lories
and the rainbow-parrots landing.
There's not a fruit on any tree
to match their crimson, green and gold.

To see them cling and sip and sway,
loquats are no great price to pay.

Betty Temple Watts (1901–1992)
Detail from *Parrots* 1958–1967
nla.pic-an6940276-7

Magpies

Along the road the magpies walk
with hands in pockets, left and right.
They tilt their heads, and stroll and talk.
In their well-fitted black and white

they look like certain gentlemen
who seem most nonchalant and wise
until their meal is served—and then
what clashing beaks, what greedy eyes!

But not one man that I have heard
throws back his head in such a song
of grace and praise—no man nor bird.
Their greed is brief; their joy is long.
For each is born with such a throat
as thanks his God with every note.

Antoine-Germain Bevalet (1779–1850)
Magpie, from 'Voyage de l'Uranie, *oiseaux, Cassican fluteur, White-backed magpie'* c.1819
nla.pic-an24283548

Lilian Medland (1880–1955)
Tawny Frogmouths; detail from *Dacelo leachii and Other Birds* 1930s
nla.pic-an14236954

Wounded Night-bird

Walking one lukewarm, lamp-black night I heard
a yard from me his harsh rattle of warning,
and in a landing-net of torchlight saw him crouch—
the devil, small but dangerous. My heart's lurch
betrayed me to myself. But I am learning:
I can distinguish: the devil is no bird.

A bird with a broken breast. But what a stare
he fronted me with!—his look abashed my own.
He was all eyes, furious, meant to wound.
And I, who meant to heal, took in my hand
his depth of down, his air-light delicate bone,
his heart in the last extreme of pain and fear.

From nerve to nerve I felt the circuit blaze.
Along my veins his anguish beat; his eyes
flared terror into mine and cancelled time,
and the black whirlpool closed over my head
and clogged my throat with the cry that knows no aid.
Far down beneath the reach of succouring light
we fought, we suffered, we were sunk in night.

Betty Temple Watts (1901–1992)
Detail from *Flycatchers and Fantails* 1958–1967
nla.pic-an6940276-21

The Wagtail

So elegant he is and neat
from round black head to slim black feet!
He sways and flirts upon the fence,
his collar clean as innocence.

The city lady looks and cries
"Oh charming bird with dewdrop eyes,
how kind of you to sing that song!"
But what a pity—she is wrong.
"Sweet-pretty-creature"—yes, but who
is the one he sings it to?
    Not me—not you.

The furry moth, the gnat perhaps,
on which his scissor-beak snip-snaps.

E.E. (Ebenezer Edward) Gostelow (1867–1944)
The Australian Pelican (Pelecanus conspicillatus) 1924
nla.pic-an3829077

Pelicans

Funnel-web spider, snake and octopus,
pitcher-plant and vampire-bat and shark—
these are cold water on an easy faith.
Look at them, but don't linger.
If we stare too long, something looks back at us;
something gazes through from underneath;
something crooks a very dreadful finger
down there in an unforgotten dark.

Turn away then, and look up at the sky.
There sails that old clever Noah's Ark,
the well-turned, well-carved pelican
with his wise comic eye;
he turns and wheels down, kind as an ambulance-driver,
to join his fleet. Pelicans rock together,
solemn as clowns in white on a circus-river,
meaning: this world holds every sort of weather.

Silver Terns

It was a morning blue as ocean's mirror,
and strong and warm the wind was blowing.
Along the shore a flock of terns went flying,
their long white wings as clean as pearl.

Inland among the boulders of grey coral
their mates upon the eggs sat waiting.
A shoal of fishes hurried by the island
and the terns plunged into the shoal.

The sea was pocked with sudden silver fountains
where the birds dived, so swift and clever;
and some rose with a flash of fish and water
as sunlight broke on splash and scale;

but some, we saw, stayed down and did not rise.
That shoal the big bonito harried,
and they took fish and diving bird together.
One tern rose like a bloodied sail,

and a bonito leapt to make its capture.
All morning it went on, that slaughter,
with white birds diving, obstinate with hunger;
and some would rise, and some would fail.

The morning was as gentle as a pearl,
the sea was pocked with sudden silver fountains;
you would not guess the blood, unless you saw it,
that the waves washed from feather and from scale.

Betty Temple Watts (1901–1992)
Detail from *Waders, Gulls and Terns* 1958–1967
nla.pic-an6940276-4

Brown Bird

Brown bird with the silver eyes,
fly down and teach me to sing.
I am alone, I will not
touch you or move.
I am only thirsty for love
and the clear stream of your voice
and the brown curve of your wing
and the cold of your silver eyes.

Yet though I hung my head
and did not look or move,
he felt my thirst and was gone.
Though not a word I said,
he would not give me a song.
My heart sounded too strong;
too desert looked my love.

E.E. (Ebenezer Edward) Gostelow (1867–1944)

Rufous Whistler (Pachycephala rufiventris) 1932

nla.pic-an3928755

Black Cockatoos

Each certain kind of weather or of light
has its own creatures. Somewhere else they wait
as though they but inhabited heat or cold,
twilight or dawn, and knew no other state.
Then at their time they come, timid or bold.

So when the long drought-winds, sandpaper-harsh,
were still, and the air changed, and the clouds came,
and other birds were quiet in prayer or fear,
these knew their hour. Before the first far flash
lit up, or the first thunder spoke its name,
in heavy flight they came, till I could hear
the wild black cockatoos, tossed on the crest
of their high trees, crying the world's unrest.

E.E. (Ebenezer Edward) Gostelow (1867–1944)

White-Tailed (or Baudin's) Black Cockatoo (Calyptorhynchus baudinii) 1929

nla.pic-an3810775

J.W. (John William) Lewin (1770–1819)
Mountain Bee-Eater; current name Rainbow Bee-Eater (Merops ornatus) 1838
nla.pic-an10496110

Rainbow-bird

Once in a winter killing as its war,
and settled in the heart as sharp as sleet,
under a trellised rose hook-thorned and bare
that twined its whips and flogged the cruel air,
the rainbow-bird lay fallen at my feet.

Yes, fallen, fallen like the spring's delight,
that bird that turned too late to find the spring.
The cold had struck him spinning from its height;
his cobweb-plumes, his breast too neat and slight
to beat that wind back, and his twisted wing.

And I stood looking. All of me was chilled.
My face was silent as a mask of wood,
and I had thought my very core was killed.
But he in his soft colours lay more cold
even than my heart. He met me like a word
I needed—pity? love?—the rainbow-bird.

Hardy Wilson (1881–1955)
Black Swan, Australia 1952
nla.pic-an2793166

Black Swans

Night after night the rounding moon
rose like a bushfire through the air.
Night after night the swans came in—
the lake at morning rocked them there.

The inland fired the western wind
from plains bared by a year-long drought.
Only the coastal lakes were kind
until that bitter year ran out.

Black swans shadowed the blaze of moon
as they came curving down the sky.
On hills of night the red stars burned
like sparks blown where the wind is high.
On rushing wings the black swans turned
sounding aloud their desolate cry.

Night Herons

It was after a day's rain:
the street facing the west
was lit with growing yellow;
the black road gleamed.

First one child looked and saw
and told another.
Face after face, the windows
flowered with eyes.

It was like a long fuse lighted,
the news travelling.
No one called out loudly;
everyone said "Hush."

The light deepened; the wet road
answered in daffodil colours,
and down its centre
walked the two tall herons.

Stranger than wild birds, even,
what happened on those faces:
suddenly believing in something,
they smiled and opened.

Children thought of fountains,
circuses, swans feeding;
women remembered words
spoken when they were young.

Everyone said "Hush;"
no one spoke loudly;
but suddenly the herons
rose and were gone. The light faded.

Lionel Lindsay (1874–1961)
Night Heron 1935
nla.pic-an10889642

Lyrebirds

Over the west side of this mountain,
that's lyrebird country.
I could go down there, they say, in the early morning,
and I'd see them, I'd hear them.

Ten years, and I have never gone.
I'll never go.
I'll never see the lyrebirds—
the few, the shy, the fabulous,
the dying poets.

I should see them, if I lay there in the dew:
first a single movement
like a waterdrop falling, then stillness,
then a brown head, brown eyes,
a splendid bird, bearing
like a crest the symbol of his art,
the high symmetrical shape of the perfect lyre.
I should hear that master practising his art.

No, I have never gone.
Some things ought to be left secret, alone;
some things—birds like walking fables—
ought to inhabit nowhere but the reverence of the heart.

Betty Temple Watts (1901–1992)
Detail of *Lyrebirds and Bower-Birds* 1958–1967
nla.pic-an6940276-17

Satin Bower-birds

In summer they can afford their independence,
down in the gullies, in the folds of forest;
but with the early frosts they're here again—
hopping like big toy birds, as round as pullets,
handsomely green and speckled, but somehow comic—
begging their bread. A domestic,
quarrelling, amateur troupe.

Ordinary birds with ordinary manners,
uninteresting as pigeons;
but, like the toad, they have a secret.
Look—the young male bird—
see his eye's perfect mineral blaze of blue.
The winter sea's not purer
than that blue flash set in a bird's head.

Then I remember
how ritually they worship that one colour.
Blue chips of glass, blue rag, blue paper,
the heads of my grape-hyacinths,
I found in their secret bower; and there are dances
done in the proper season,
for birth, initiation, marriage and perhaps death.

Seven years, some say, those green-brown birds
elect blue for their colour
and dance for it, their eyes round as the sea's horizons,
blue as grape-hyacinths.

And when those seven years are served?
See, there he flies, the old one,
the male made perfect—
black in the shadow, but in the caressing sun
bluer, more royal than the ancient sea.

Betty Temple Watts (1901–1992)
Detail of *Lyrebirds and Bower-Birds* 1958–1967
nla.pic-an6940276-17

Brush Turkey

Right to the edge of his forest
the tourists come.
He learns the scavenger's habits
with scrap and crumb—
his forests shrunk, he lives
on what the moment gives:
pretends, in mockery,
to beg our charity.

Cunning and shy one must be
to snatch one's bread
from oafs whose hands are quicker
with stones instead.
He apes the backyard bird;
half-proud and half-absurd,
sheltered by his quick wit,
he sees and takes his bit.

Ash-black, wattles of scarlet,
and careful eye,
he hoaxes the ape, the ogre,
with mimicry.
Scornfully, he will eat
thrown crust and broken meat
till suddenly—"See, oh see!
The turkey's in the tree."

The backyard bird is stupid;
he trusts and takes.
But this one's wiles are wary
to guard against the axe:
escaping, neat and pat,
into his habitat.
Charred log and shade and stone
accept him. He is gone.

And here's a bird the poet
may ponder over,
whose ancient forest-meanings
no longer grant him cover;
who, circumspect yet proud,
like yet unlike the crowd,
must cheat its chucklehead
to throw—not stones, but bread.

E.E. (Ebenezer Edward) Gostelow (1867–1944)
Brush Turkey (Alectura lathami) 1939
nla.pic-an3927338

E.E. (Ebenezer Edward) Gostelow (1867–1944)
Koel (Eudynamis orientalis) 1932
nla.pic-an3922557

The Koel

One spring when life itself was happiness,
he called and called across the orange-trees
his two strange syllables; and clouds of perfume
followed along the hesitating breeze.

And when he calls, the spring has come again,
and the old joy floods up in memory.
Yet his sad foster-kin cannot forget
the wrong he does them—Cain from his infancy.

Dark wary rebel, migrant without a home
except the spring, bird whom so many hate,
voice of one tune and only one—yet come.
In fear yet boldly, come and find your mate.
Against their anger, outcast by them all,
choose your one love and call your single call—
the endless tale you cannot cease to tell,
half-question, half-reply—*Koel! Koel!*

Dotterel

Wild and impermanent
as the sea-foam blown,
the dotterel keeps its distance
and runs alone.

Bare beach, salt wind,
its loved solitude,
hold all that it asks
of shelter and food.

I saw its single egg
dropped on the sand,
with neither straw nor wall
to warm or defend;

and the new-hatched chick,
like a thistle's pale down,
fled and crouched quiet
as sand or as stone.

Water's edge, land's edge
and edge of the air—
the dotterel chooses
to live nowhere.

It runs, but not in fear;
and its thin high call
is like a far bugle
that troubles the soul.

E.E. (Ebenezer Edward) Gostelow (1867–1944)
Australian Dotterel (Peltohyas australis) 1933
nla.pic-an3819218

Lory

On the bough of blue summer
hangs one crimson berry.
Like the blood of a lover
is the breast of the lory.

The blood-drinking butcher-birds
pray and sing together.
They long to gather from his breast
the red of one feather.

But "The heart's red is my reward,"
the old crow cries
"I'll wear his colour on my black
the day the lory dies."

William T. Cooper (1934–)
Yellow-Bibbed, Purple-Naped and White-Naped Lory 1970
nla.pic–an4084188

Extinct Birds

Charles Harpur in his journals long ago
(written in hope and love, and never printed)
recorded the birds of his time's forest—
birds long vanished with the fallen forest—
described in copperplate on unread pages.

The scarlet satin-bird, swung like a lamp in berries,
he watched in love, and then in hope described it.
There was a bird, blue, small, spangled like dew.
All now are vanished with the fallen forest.
And he, unloved, past hope, was buried,

who helped with proud stained hands to fell the forest,
and set those birds in love on unread pages;
yet thought himself immortal, being a poet.
And is he not immortal, where I found him,
in love and hope along his careful pages?—
the poet vanished, in the vanished forest,
among his brightly tinted extinct birds?

above: Anna Maria Lewin (died c.1846)
High Flyer of New Holland 1826
nla.pic-an6939245

left: Unknown photographer
Portrait of Charles Harpur (1813–1868) c.1860s
nla.pic-an23436164

SUPPLEMENTARY POEMS

Lilian Medland (1880–1955)
Detail from *Providence Petrel (Pterodroma solandri)* 1930s
nla.pic-an10710503

Camping at Split Rock

Red mounting scales of cliff lead the eye up;
but here the rock has spaces of tenderness
where light and water open its heart. A lip
of narrow green shows where the creek-banks bless
a niche for trees and birds. So many birds!
Outside our tent they cross and recross our patch
of vision, hatch the air and double-hatch
in diving curves and lines. Each curve has words;

each flight speaks its own bird. The slowly strong
deep-thrusting heron's stroke; the glittering
daring rush of the swallow and the long
poise and turn of hawk on a still wing;
the quick low scuttle of wren, the coloured wind
of finches, blue jays wide noble rise and fall—
we read each bird from its air-written scrawl,
the bird no stranger than the interpreting mind.

The finger of age-old water splits the rock
and makes us room to live; the age-old word
runs on in language and from obstinate dark
hollows us room for seeing. The birds go by;
but we can name and hold them, each a word
that crystals round a more than mortal bird.

— From *The Other Half*, 1966

Brown Goshawk

Little Eagle   light phase

Little Eagle   dark phase

Black-shouldered Kite

Whistling Eagle

Fork-tailed Kite

Kestrel

Brown Hawk   light phase

Peregrine Falcon

Brown Hawk   dark phase

Swamp Harrier

Spotted   Harrier

B·T·W
1960

Betty Temple Watts (1901–1992)
Diurnal Birds-of-Prey 1958–1967
nla.pic-an6940276-30

E.E. (Ebenezer Edward) Gostelow (1867–1944)

Olive-Backed Oriole (Oriolus sagittatus) 1937

nla.pic–an3923181

Oriole, Oriole

Picking narcissus in the long grass
of the fenced acre by my house,
for twenty years long I stilled and heard
in the blackbean tree that greenvoiced bird,
Oriole is his singing name,
his wings a green stir in the green.
Oriole, oriole,
I whistle you up, I wait to hear.
No orioles sing to me this year.

Does poison creep through earth or air?
Did the last nest fall with a felled tree?
Has every oriole gone away
and left my acre lonely?
Nor a stirring heard or seen
of green wing, green melody.
Oriole, oriole,
I whistle you up, my green-in-green,
but day after silent day
you leave my acre lonely.

— From *Alive*, 1973

73

Lament for Passenger Pigeons

("Don't ask for the meaning, ask for the use." —Wittgenstein)

The voice of water as it flows and falls
the noise air makes against earth-surfaces
have changed; are changing to the tunes we choose.

What wooed and echoed in the pigeon's voice?
We have not heard the bird. How reinvent
that passenger, its million wings and hues,

when we have lost the bird, the thing itself,
the sheen of life on flashing long migrations?
Might human musics hold it, could we hear?

Trapped in the fouling nests of time and space,
we turn the music on; but it is man,
and it is man who leans a deafening ear.

And it is man we eat and man we drink
and man who thickens round us like a stain.
Ice at the polar axis smells of me.

A word, a class, a formula, a use:
that is the rhythm, the cycle we impose.
The sirens sang us to the ends of sea,

and changed to us; their voices were our own,
jug-jug to dirty ears in dirtied brine.
Pigeons and angels sang us to the sky

and turned to metal and a dirty need.
The height of sky, the depth of sea we are,
sick with a yellow stain, a fouling dye.

Whatever Being is, that formula,
it dies as we pursue it past the word.
We have not asked the meaning, but the use.

What is the use of water when it dims?
The use of air that whines an emptiness?
The use of glass-eyed pigeons caged in glass?

We listen to the sea, that old machine,
to air that hoarsens on earth-surfaces
and has no angel, no migrating cry.

What is the being and the end of man?
Blank surfaces reverb a human voice
whose echo tells us that we choose to die:

or else, against the blank of everything,
to reinvent that passenger, that bird-
siren-and-angel image we contain
essential in a constellating word.
To sing of Being, its escaping wing,
to utter absence in a human chord
and recreate the meaning as we sing.

— From *Alive*, 1973

Reminiscence

I was born into a coloured country;
spider-webs in dew on feathered grass,
mountains blue as wrens,
valleys cupping sky in like a cradle,
christmas-beetles winged with buzzing opal;
finches, robins, gang-gangs, pardalotes
tossed the blossom in its red-streaked trees.

My father had a tale of an old neighbour,
the kind of reminiscence one inherits.
Asked for difficult detail in his stories
at those bygone ample crowded teas,
(cup and saucer balanced on his knees):
"Madam, you might as well
ask me to enumerate the parrots."

Hundreds, thousands, birds uncountable
babbling, shrieking, swirling all around—
skiesful, treesful: lorikeets, rosellas,
lorilets and cockatiels and lowries,
Red-backed, Ring-necked, Orange-breasted, Turquoise,
Purple-crowned, Red-collared, Rainbow, Varied,
Scarlet-chested, Blue-browed, Scalybreasted,
Swift and Night and Paradise and Crimson,
Twenty-eight and Red-capped, Musk and Elegant—
I give up. But see him
sitting stiffly in a basket-chair
circled by their millions, formally

stirring three of sugar in his tea
in an afternoon I never knew
making conversation with the ladies.

Not a flock of parrots left to number.
Just a picture, fifty years behind,
left embroidered on my childish mind.
Parrots! They were something to remember.

— From *Alive*, 1973

Betty Temple Watts (1901–1992)
Gang-Gang Cockatoos; detail from *Lorikeets and Cockatoos* 1958
nla.pic-an6940276-6

Seasonal Flocking

Last week outside my window
the tree grew red rosellas,
berry-bright fruits, the young ones
brocaded with juvenile green.
I said, the autumn's ending.
They have come out of the mountains
and the snowcloud shadows.

This week on the road to town
in the red-hung hawthorn,
eleven of the Twelve Apostles;
eight black cockatoos, their tails
fanned to show yellow panes,
uncounted magpies and currawongs
greasily fat from the dump and the butcher's
throwouts—
that breeding-ground of maggots.

All of them flocked together,
crying aloud, knowing
the end of autumn.
Sharp-edged welcome-swallows
gathered and circled upwards.

Frost soon, and the last warmth passes.
Seed-stems rot on wet grasses.

At the end of autumn
I too—I want you near me,
all you who've gone, who scatter
into far places or are hidden under
summer-forgotten gravestones.

— From *Phantom Dwelling*, 1985

Betty Temple Watts (1901–1992)
Red-Rumped Parrots; detail from *Parrots* 1958–1967
nla.pic-an6940276-7

Notes on the Artists

Antoine-Germain Bevalet (1779–1850) p. 35: magpie drawn from live specimen brought back to France from voyage of *l'Uranie* (1817–1820) captained by Louis de Freycinet.

Neville Henry Cayley (1853–1903) pp. 11, 13: born England. Early promoter of distinctiveness of Australian birdlife. *Australian Birds: A Beautiful Coloured Series* (11 plates; NSW Bookstall, 1900). His children Neville William Cayley (*What Bird is That?*; A&R, 1947) and Alice Cayley were also bird painters.

William T. Cooper (b.1934) p. 65: Queensland natural history artist and illustrator; art teacher. This image comes from *Parrots of the World* (Lansdowne, 1973).

E.E. (Ebenezer Edward) Gostelow (1867–1944) pp. 17, 19, 25, 30, 40, 45, 47, 59, 60, 63, 72: with no artistic training began to paint native flora and fauna while teaching at Broken Hill and Harden (NSW), later redrawing earlier, 'inaccurate' works, with the aim of depicting all species of birds on the continent.

J.W. (John William) Lewin (1770–1819) and **Anna Maria Lewin (died c.1846)** pp. 48 and 67 respectively: John Lewin, English artist, naturalist and engraver. Arrived Sydney 1800. *Birds of New South Wales* (1808, 1813, 1822, 1838)—the first illustrated publication made here. Anna Maria Lewin, illustrator, was his wife.

Lionel Lindsay (1874–1961) pp. 9, 53: artist and journalist, contributed black-and-white drawings to Sydney *Bulletin* and other magazines. Later celebrated for watercolours, etchings, and particularly his woodcuts of Australian animals and birds.

Lilian Marguerite Medland (1880–1955) pp. 14, 22, 36, 69: emigrated from London 1923, married ornithologist Tom Iredale. Work appeared in Gregory Macalister Mathews' *A Manual of the Birds of Australia* (1921), and in Iredale's *Birds of Paradise and Bower Birds* (1950) and *Birds of New Guinea* (1956). Also painted birds for Australian Museum (Sydney).

Betty Temple Watts (1901–1992) pp. 21, 27, 29, 33, 38, 43, 55, 57, 71, 77, 79: migrated to Australia 1942. Drew birds for stamp series (Australian Post Office, 1964), and for Australian section of British Ornithologists' Union's *The New Dictionary of Birds*. Watercolours reproduced here come from 35 plates painted 1958–1967 for *Birds in the Australian High Country* (A.H. & A.W. Reed, 1969).

Hardy Wilson (1881–1955) p. 50: architect, artist, writer and thinker best known for drawings of early colonial Georgian-style buildings. Swan reproduced here was to feature on library in Wilson's designs for an eastern-influenced future city he named Kurrajong.